SAN FRANCISCO 2013

THE CITY AT A GLANCE

Transamerica Pyramid
At 260m tall, the city's mo
skyscraper towers over th
It's no longer home to the
corporation, but the nam
See p013

City Hall
A Beaux Arts gem topped
this central building of the
to be restored after the 1989 earthquake.
It was reopened in 1999 in all its former glory.
1 Dr Carlton B Goodlett Place

Ferry Building
Until the 1930s, this was the main arrival
point in the city. Today, it is the location
of a vast marketplace selling fresh local
meat, cheese and assorted produce.
The Embarcadero/Market Street

Market Street
Running diagonally north-east from The
Castro up to the Ferry Building, Market
Street is a major route for the city's fleet
of renovated 1950s cable cars.

SFMOMA
Its distinctive stripes and looming 'eye'
still impress, and Mario Botta's San Francisco
Museum of Modern Art, one of the first
'destination' galleries in the US when it
opened in 1995, promises big things with
its upcoming expansion, due in 2016.
See p037

Bay Bridge
One of the longest bridges in the world, this
is actually two spans in one, joined by Yerba
Buena Island. Its cantilevered eastern half,
damaged in the 1989 earthquake, is being
completely rebuilt and will open in 2013.

INTRODUCTION
THE CHANGING FACE OF THE URBAN SCENE

One of the most cosmopolitan of all the cities in the United States, San Francisco is blessed with a laidback, liberal mindset and a dramatic setting that only adds to its allure. This is an enthralling city of contradictions: traditional architecture and directional new buildings sit side by side; 1950s cable cars share the streets with 21st-century hybrid vehicles; old-world museums stand next to concept gallery spaces; and there's a cheeriness in the locals that belies the fact that their home sits atop a volatile fault line.

Less daunting and aggressive than New York, and more compact than Los Angeles, San Francisco is relatively straightforward to navigate (although, as in most US cities, it helps to have a car). Couple this with the way its diverse tribes stick to well-defined neighbourhoods, and you should be able to see the place from your preferred angle without too much trouble. The old-money mansions of Pacific Heights look to past glories, in contrast to emerging districts such as Dogpatch, which are ushering in a new era of creativity. An exuberant food scene is marshalled by the country's most adventurous (and youngest) chefs, including Danny Bowien at <u>Mission Chinese Food</u> (2234 Mission Street, T 863 2800) and <u>Locanda Osteria</u>'s Anthony Strong (see p050). At the same time, new museums designed by Renzo Piano and Daniel Libeskind have joined buildings by Morphosis and Rafael Viñoly, all of which have increased the city's global presence.

ESSENTIAL INFO

FACTS, FIGURES AND USEFUL ADDRESSES

TOURIST OFFICE
900 Market Street
T 391 2000
www.sanfrancisco.travel

TRANSPORT
Cable cars and trolleybuses
Muni
www.sfmuni.com
Services run from roughly 6am to 1am
Car hire
Avis
T 929 2555
Helicopter
San Francisco Helicopter Tours
T 650 635 4500
www.sfhelicoptertours.com
Taxis
Yellow Cab Cooperative
T 333 3333
It's easy and safe to hail a cab on the street
Trains
Bay Area Rapid Transit
www.bart.gov
Trains run until midnight; from 4am on
weekdays, 6am Saturday and 8am Sunday

EMERGENCY SERVICES
Emergencies
T 911
24-hour pharmacy
Walgreens
459 Powell Street
T 984 0793
www.walgreens.com

CONSULATE
British Consulate-General
1 Sansome Street
Suite 850
T 617 1300
www.ukinusa.fco.gov.uk

POSTAL SERVICES
Post office
150 Sutter Street
T 765 1761
Shipping
UPS
T 775 6644

BOOKS
**A Crack in the Edge of the World: The
Great American Earthquake of 1906**
by Simon Winchester (Penguin)
Tales of the City
by Armistead Maupin (Black Swan)
This is San Francisco
by Miroslav Sasek (Universe)

WEBSITES
Art/Design
www.fecalface.com
www.sfarts.org
Newspaper
www.sfgate.com

EVENTS
San Francisco Design Week
www.sfdesignweek.org
**San Francisco International
Film Festival**
www.sffs.org

COST OF LIVING
Taxi from SFO Airport to city centre
$50
Cappuccino
$4
Packet of cigarettes
$7
Daily newspaper
$1
Bottle of champagne
$75

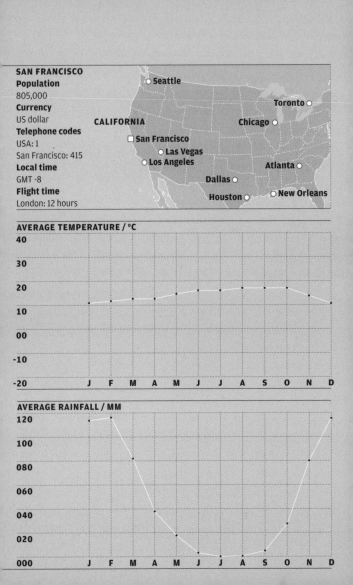

SAN FRANCISCO
Population
805,000
Currency
US dollar
Telephone codes
USA: 1
San Francisco: 415
Local time
GMT -8
Flight time
London: 12 hours

Seattle
Toronto
CALIFORNIA
Chicago
San Francisco
Las Vegas
Los Angeles
Atlanta
Dallas
Houston
New Orleans

AVERAGE TEMPERATURE / °C

	J	F	M	A	M	J	J	A	S	O	N	D
40												
30												
20												
10												
00												
-10												
-20												

AVERAGE RAINFALL / MM

	J	F	M	A	M	J	J	A	S	O	N	D
120												
100												
080												
060												
040												
020												
000												

NEIGHBOURHOODS
THE AREAS YOU NEED TO KNOW AND WHY

To help you navigate the city, we've chosen the most interesting districts (see below and the map inside the back cover) and colour-coded our featured venues, according to their location; those venues that are outside these areas are not coloured.

NORTH BEACH
Home to countless restaurants and bars, North Beach and Telegraph Hill are in the city's north-east corner, where the hilltop art deco Coit Tower (see p010) keeps a beady eye on proceedings. Most theatres and comedy venues are to be found here.

NOB HILL
This is where the gold and silver barons flocked in the 1800s, to be above the hoi polloi. The neighbourhood looks over the Financial District, Russian Hill and the Bay, and is home to The Fairmont hotel (see p016) and Grace Cathedral (1100 California Street, T 749 6300).

HAIGHT-ASHBURY
Surely the most famous cross street in the US, Haight-Ashbury is now a sad pastiche, with relics from its psychedelic heyday and teens in tie-dye searching for ghosts of the beatniks and the Grateful Dead. A few stores have tried to reinvent the area, but it's best remembered for what it once stood for, not what it has become.

SOMA
South of Market Street, or SoMa, is the city's cultural epicentre, encompassing SFMOMA (see p037), the Museum of the African Diaspora (685 Mission Street, T 358 7200) and the Yerba Buena Center for the Arts (701 Mission Street, T 978 2700) in the east, as well as the 2007 Federal Building (see p014) and some great hotels.

CHINATOWN
A bustling downtown hub, this is the largest Chinatown in the US. From its iconic gate and alleys, to the fine Sichuan cuisine — found at Z&Y (655 Jackson Street, T 981 8988) — its crowded streets are fairly contained and fascinating to roam.

THE CASTRO
As the heart of the West Coast's gay scene, The Castro seems too outré to be true. But this is the most liberal neighbourhood in America's most liberal city, so leave your prejudices at the door and enjoy the show. Unsurprisingly, it's home to some of the best clubs and bars, so do explore a little.

THE MISSION
San Francisco's hottest artists, hippest bars and edgiest boutiques are all in this most creative district. Look out for quirky restaurants, such as Mission Chinese Food (2234 Mission Street, T 863 2800). The area is named after the Spanish Mission Dolores, the city's oldest building; the Latino community here remains strong.

HAYES VALLEY
Located between the Civic Center to the east and Alamo Square to the west, this fashionable area centres on Hayes Street, where the city's most innovative shops are located, including the florist-cum-magazine store Birch (564 Hayes Street, T 626 6860). One of the better-known eateries here is Sebo (see p053).

LANDMARKS
THE SHAPE OF THE CITY SKYLINE

San Francisco is something of a landmark itself, for everything it suggests and personifies about the American psyche. Imbued with cool and charm, it's also a sight to behold, when viewed from either the Bay or the monumental Golden Gate Bridge (see p012) with the Californian sun illuminating its buildings. Driving up and down the city's rollercoaster streets, it's easy to understand why Steve McQueen's Frank Bullitt, racing along in his green Mustang, is hailed as the coolest cop ever to appear on screen.

Hemmed in on three sides by water, San Francisco has always grown vertically – the only way it could. As a result, the quirky splendour of the 19th-century architecture that survived the calamitous 1906 earthquake (most of the city was destroyed by the time the ensuing fire was put out) has since been swallowed up downtown by bland, formulaic skyscrapers. Standing out from the crowd, however, is William L Pereira's gleaming, quartz-fronted Transamerica Pyramid (see p013); it can be seen from most parts of the city, acting as a useful orientation point.

This city has its fair share of unusual landmarks too. For instance, Lombard Street (see p034) draws coachloads of tourists to wonder at its sine-wave windings. And although the Dutch Windmill at Ocean Beach (1691 John F Kennedy Drive) is not as well known internationally, it's still beloved by locals.

For full addresses, see Resources.

Coit Tower

The 64m art deco Coit Tower stands on top of Telegraph Hill's Pioneer Park, and affords visitors some of the finest views of the Bay from its top rotunda. Built using funds left to the city by a wealthy financier's widow, Lillie Hitchcock Coit, it was finished in 1933. Inside, local artists have created murals that depict the Great Depression. *1 Telegraph Hill Boulevard, T 362 0808*

Golden Gate Bridge

One of the world's great architectural icons, the Golden Gate Bridge is instantly recognisable and, when seen first-hand, its power remains undiminished. The 2.7km structure spans the Pacific Ocean where it meets San Francisco Bay, its two giant towers rising 227m above the water. Finished in 1937, the bridge was originally going to be painted black and yellow, but the project's guiding architect, Irving F Morrow, insisted on the now-irreplaceable international orange. The structure seems to accentuate its own myth, as it is often shrouded in fog rolling in off the ocean, or bathed in dappled Californian sunshine. Driving across it in a convertible is surely on everyone's must-do list.

T 921 5858, www.goldengatebridge.org

Transamerica Pyramid

William L Pereira's 48-floor pyramid, which was completed in 1972, dominates the Financial District and beyond, and is a useful pointer for getting your bearings in the city. Nicknamed Pereira's Prick by its detractors, it faced fierce opposition during its planning and construction, but is now as identifiable with San Francisco as the Golden Gate Bridge. The building is covered in crushed quartz, which gives it a white appearance, and viewed from over the bay on a sunny day, it does seem to glow. After the 9/11 attacks, an observation deck near the top was closed, but large screens in the lobby display views from cameras mounted at the top of the spire. *600 Montgomery Street, www.thepyramidcenter.com*

Federal Building

This soaring federal HQ, completed in 2007 by architects Morphosis, who were also behind the brutalist Caltrans District 7 HQ in downtown LA, towers over the SoMa district. The most radical build in the heart of the city for decades, it has divided locals as to whether it is an icon or an eyesore. In 2008 it won a Design Award from the city's AIA chapter.
Mission Street/7th Street

HOTELS
WHERE TO STAY AND WHICH ROOMS TO BOOK

For all of San Francisco's liberal leanings, its hotels remain a conservative bunch. Despite the relatively recent additions of the St Regis (see p025) and InterContinental (see p030), as well as the renovations of established names such as the Phoenix (601 Eddy Street, T 776 1380) and the Mandarin Oriental (222 Sansome Street, T 276 9888), there is nothing to rival the daring concepts of, say, the Petit Moulin in Paris or Madrid's Hotel Puerta América. That said, with classic offerings, such as the Palace Hotel (see p029) and The Fairmont (950 Mason Street, T 772 5000), still taking up residence in the city, perhaps no one feels the need to deviate from the hundred-year-old formula.

Nearly all the better hotels are to be found in the east, from the vast, splendid old mansion blocks of Nob Hill to the business-and-conference chains along Market Street and The Embarcadero, and the modernist elegance of the newer builds in SoMa. The Orchard Garden (466 Bush Street, T 399 9807), the city's first eco-friendly hotel, was built to conform to US Green Building Council guidelines, although this does not compromise the level of luxury that one expects from a destination hotel. However, as The Mission continues to gentrify, it's surely only a matter of time before a forward-thinking hotelier seizes the initiative and opens a boutique establishment in this up-and-coming area.
For full addresses and room rates, see Resources.

Dear Reader, books by Phaidon are recognized worldwide for their beauty, scholarship and elegance. We invite you to return this card with your name and e-mail address so that we can keep you informed of our new publications, special offers and events. Alternatively, visit us at **www.phaidon.com** to see our entire list of books, videos and stationery. Register on-line to be included on our regular e-newsletters.

Subjects in which I have a special interest

☐ General Non-Fiction ☐ Art ☐ Photography ☐ Architecture ☐ Design

☐ Fashion ☐ Music ☐ Children's ☐ Food ☐ Travel

	Mr/Miss/Ms	Initial	Surname
Name	⎿⎿⎿⎿⎿⎿⎿⎿⎿⎿⎿⎿⎿⎿⎿⎿⎿		
No./Street	⎿⎿⎿⎿⎿⎿⎿⎿⎿⎿⎿⎿⎿⎿⎿⎿⎿		
City	⎿⎿⎿⎿⎿⎿⎿⎿⎿⎿⎿⎿⎿⎿⎿⎿⎿		
Postcode/Zip code	⎿⎿⎿⎿⎿⎿⎿⎿⎿⎿ Country ⎿⎿⎿⎿⎿⎿⎿		
E-mail	⎿⎿⎿⎿⎿⎿⎿⎿⎿⎿⎿⎿⎿⎿⎿⎿⎿		

This is not an order form. To order please contact Customer Services at the appropriate address overleaf.

Please delete address not required before mailing

PHAIDON PRESS LIMITED

Regent's Wharf

All Saints Street

London N1 9PA

UK

PHAIDON PRESS INC.

180 Varick Street

New York

NY 10014

USA

Return address for USA and Canada only

Return address for UK and countries
outside the USA and Canada only

Mystic Hotel

Although it opened in 2009 (as The Crescent), and was refurbished in 2012, the Mystic Hotel feels as if it's been in its shabby-chic Victorian building for a century. Rooms, such as the Mystic Junior Suite (above), feature minibars stocked with wine from small Californian labels, and a nicely curated selection of dog-eared classic books amid chandeliers, original wainscoting and bay windows.

Locals are also known to swing by and visit the tucked-away bar, the Burritt Room, which has raw brick walls and worn leather sofas. Named after the Nob Hill alley where Miles Archer was murdered in *The Maltese Falcon*, it serves up highfalutin cocktails, without the scrum of other area drinkeries.
417 Stockton Street, T 400 0500,
www.mystichotel.com

W

Located next door to SFMOMA (see
p037), this is arguably the most design-
forward hotel in San Francisco. The rooms
are splashed with bright blues, vibrant
oranges and funky patterned upholstery
and can be as flamboyant as the 65 sq m
Fantastic Suite (opposite), which features
a living room and two baths. Otherwise,
opt for one of the more introspective Cool
Corner Rooms, which have cozy dark
wood panelling and Chinese-inspired
wall art, and, in some, views over the Yerba
Buena Gardens. Elsewhere, cocktails are
served in the Stanley Saitowitz-designed
Living Room Bar; its fireplace and lounge
area (above) are equally inviting. If the
party downstairs and bustling street
scenes outside get too much, relax with
a pampering treatment at the Bliss Spa
(T 877 862 5477) or in the indoor lap pool.
181 3rd Street, T 777 5300,
www.wsanfrancisco.com

The Huntington Hotel

Perched atop Nob Hill, The Huntington is one of San Francisco's most famous hotels. Its majestic sign, stretching several metres into the sky, can be seen from most points in the city, and its brick exterior gives it the air of a knowing grande dame. This hotel has more of a European feel than any other in the city, which might explain why the majority of its guests seem to hail from outside the United States. Don't let the lobby, tiny elevators or narrow hallways fool you; the rooms are, for the most part, more like studio apartments than hotel accommodation, as with the Mulholland Suite (above), and feature wonderful views of the city. The Huntington is known to have a few duds in its room catalogue, so it's best to be specific when booking. *1075 California Street, T 474 5400, www.huntingtonhotel.com*

Hotel Vertigo

After a $5m renovation, Hotel York re-emerged as Hotel Vertigo in 2009, taking its new name from the Hitchcock film that made the location famous (Kim Novak's character lived in the building). Vertigo is a delightfully whimsical choice, combining a white, orange and aubergine palette with oversized furniture, pop-art sculptures mixed with antiques, and horsehead lamps and white lacquered tables, as in the Executive King (above); the interiors feel a bit like the Mad Hatter has designed them, but in a tasteful way. The Vertigo should be applauded for taking the Hitchcock theme and running with it: art inspired by the film graces the walls, and the lobby features a large flat-screen television that shows *Vertigo* 24/7. *940 Sutter Street, T 885 6800, www.hotelvertigosf.com*

Hotel Frank
Formerly the Maxwell, Hotel Frank reopened in 2009 after a multimillion-dollar makeover. Just steps away from Union Square, this boutique hotel has been designed with a mix of 1930s art deco and contemporary decor and furnishings. The Deluxe Queen Room (pictured) is particularly spacious.
386 Geary Sreet, T 986 2000, www.hotelfranksf.com

Clift

The Clift's 19th-century exterior belies the fact that, inside, Philippe Starck and hotelier Ian Schrager have gone to town in trademark fashion. Oversized furniture and dramatic throws pepper the lobby, which opens on to the Velvet Room restaurant (T 929 2300), and the jaw-dropping Redwood Room (T 929 2372), one of the most impressive watering holes in the city. The rooms are Starck stark, decorated in shades of lavender and grey, but comfortable and elegant nonetheless, and each comes with nice touches such as a state-of-the-art sound system and luxuriant down bedding. The standard rooms, such as Room 309 (above) are pleasant, but Studio Rooms are more spacious and better value.
495 Geary Street, T 775 4700,
www.clifthotel.com

St Regis

Opened in November 2005, the St Regis is a departure from its sister hotels. Located in the heart of the burgeoning cultural quarter SoMa, the establishment boasts its own $3.5m art collection, an award-winning restaurant, Ame (T 284 4040), the world-class Remède Spa (T 284 4060) and a butler service, setting new standards in pared-down opulence. Grain-matched dark Mozambique hardwood lines all the hallways, and 2.5m doors open on to light-filled rooms with pale stitched-leather walls, crisp linens, and computerised bedside control panels. The eighth-floor Superior Rooms (above) offer postcard views. *125 3rd Street, T 284 4000, www.stregissanfrancisco.com*

Hotel Vitale

A 200-room luxury venture located at the eastern end of Mission Street, directly opposite the Ferry Building on the waterfront, the Vitale opened in 2005. Accommodation ranges from Deluxe City View Rooms to the Cielo Terrace Suite, which has a large private terrace (pictured) overlooking the Bay. Most of the rooms are bright and flooded with sunlight, and the decor is minimalist and chic. The hotel is geared towards helping guests relax: there are free daily yoga classes, two rooftop hot tubs where you can soak away the day's stresses, and the penthouse Spa Vitale (T 278 3788). There's also an excellent bar/restaurant, Americano (T 278 3777), which gets packed on week nights.
8 Mission Street, T 278 3700,
www.hotelvitale.com

Taj Campton Place

This venerable boutique hotel became one of only three Taj Hotels in the US in 2007, and the high-end Indian brand has been slowly sprucing up the place ever since. The 110 modern rooms and suites, some with stunning views of nearby Union Square, are done out in warm earth tones and soothing creams, and culminate in the top-floor Luxury Suite 1702 (above), which includes a private library and dining room. The restaurant, which offers local Californian cuisine with a Mediterranean spin, was awarded a Michelin star in 2011. Helmed by Srijith Gopinathan, it's reliably elegant, but savvy locals tend to hit the hotel's bistro and bar, one of the city's best-kept secrets, revered for its classic burgers. *340 Stockton Street, T 781 5555, www.tajhotels.com*

Palace Hotel

One of the oldest and most beautiful hotels in the city, the Palace, like The Fairmont (see p016), weathered the great quake of 1906 and, thanks to some serious renovations, now looks as splendid as it did when it first opened in 1875. Even if you're not a guest here, the spectacular 80,000-pane stained-glass atrium of The Garden Court, replete with chandeliers and marble columns, is a must-see. There are 553 rooms, including 34 suites, such as the Chancellor (above), and although they don't match the grandeur of the atrium, they do boast four-poster beds, plush fabrics and tasteful art. The in-house Pied Piper Bar & Grill (T 546 5020) is adorned with a Maxfield Parrish mural, entitled *The Pied Piper of Hamelin*. *2 New Montgomery Street, T 512 1111, www.sfpalace.com*

InterContinental

Towering over the SoMa district is the InterContinental, one of the greenest buildings in California, where solar panels generate power and an aluminium-clad exterior aids climate control. Inside, floor-to-ceiling windows on each floor not only maximise natural light but also provide stunning views throughout and act as centrepieces to the otherwise fairly simple 550 rooms. We recommend the One-Bedroom Corner Suite 3006 (above). The lobby (opposite) is similarly minimalist and plays host to Bar 888, which specialises in grappa and is often packed with the local after-work crowd. The restaurant can be skipped, but the spa, staffed by some of the best masseuses in town, is not to be missed. *888 Howard Street, T 616 6500, www.intercontinentalsanfrancisco.com*

24 HOURS

SEE THE BEST OF THE CITY IN JUST ONE DAY

San Francisco has much to offer the visitor, and its relatively small size makes it manageable to get around. You can traverse the city by car in approximately 30 minutes, so don't be afraid to venture out of the neighbourhood you're staying in and explore. The public transit system here is pretty efficient, and, as an alternative to 21st-century transportation, old cable cars and trolleybuses offer a historic way to cross town. Few cities have the luxury of being perched on a bay, so if the weather's not blowing up a squall, take in the views from the water as well as the land.

Start the day with a shot of espresso at Sightglass (opposite), before heading out for our suggested itinerary. The hairpin bends of Lombard Street (see p034) are fun to drive around on your way to the bustling Fisherman's Wharf, where the ferries to Alcatraz (see p035) depart. The Rock in the Bay is a tourist mecca, but still a fascinating place to visit, not least for the skyline view on the return journey. Once back on shore, have lunch at The Slanted Door (see p036) on Pier 1 and then visit SFMOMA (see p037); both are city essentials. The perfect way to unwind in the evening is by sampling chef Michael Tusk's locally sourced cuisine at Quince (see p038), before calling in at Top of the Mark (InterContinental Mark Hopkins, 1 Nob Hill, T 616 6916), and surveying the city with a top-notch Martini in your hand.
For full addresses, see Resources.

08.30 Sightglass

One of the newer additions to the city's infamously cultish coffee scene, Sightglass was launched by brothers Jerad and Justin Morrison in 2009. Initially working out of a humble espresso kiosk, the siblings gradually transformed the surrounding building into a coffee roastery and café, unveiling the finished venue in 2011. The industrial, raw-wood and rugged-steel interior, conceived by local designers Boor Bridges, centres on a massive iron Probat roaster, from whence come the citrusy, sustainably sourced beans. There's no wi-fi here, so, to accompany the best macchiato in the city, order a pistachio and blackberry-jam croissant, supplied by baker Greg Mindel of Neighbor, then unplug, sit back and enjoy.
270 7th Street, T 861 1313,
www.sightglasscoffee.com

10.00 Lombard Street

After breakfast, head to legendary Lombard Street (which is one-way), and twist your path down the 'crookedest street in the United States', because you have to do it at least once. Lombard's snake-like shape was created in 1922, at the suggestion of San Francisco real-estate owner and businessman Carl Henry, to tackle the steep hill's natural 27-degree slope, which presented big problems for vehicles and pedestrians who were used to more manageable 16-degree inclines. If you don't drive down, the best view is from Leavenworth Street at the bottom, looking up (above).

10.30 Alcatraz

Make your way to Fisherman's Wharf early, before it starts heaving with tourists, and board a ferry to Alcatraz – it's wise to reserve a ticket in advance as they get booked up quickly, especially in peak season. The tours of the famous prison complex in the Bay offer moving audio accounts of prisoners' lives there, and once on the island, you understand how impossible escape was, as jagged cliffs and shark-infested waters awaited anyone cunning enough to have slipped out of their cell. The views alone, looking back towards the city from the island, also known as The Rock, merit the trip. *Alcatraz Cruises, Pier 33, Hornblower Alcatraz Landing, T 981 7625, www.alcatrazcruises.com*

12.30 The Slanted Door

One of the most acclaimed restaurants in a city well known for its food, The Slanted Door played a major role in America's Asian fusion food revolution. Reportedly, the buzz around the eaterie was born when Bill and Chelsea Clinton showed up for lunch at what was then a small and relatively unknown Vietnamese venue in The Mission. Today the restaurant occupies a lovely, and much larger, spot on The Embarcadero, overlooking the water. The menu has stayed pretty much the same over the years (try the roasted mussels with kaffir lime, lemongrass and red curry broth), as executive chef and owner Charles Phan combines his Chinese roots with his childhood in Vietnam, and California's best seasonal ingredients.
1 Ferry Building No 3, T 861 8032, www.slanteddoor.com

14.00 SFMOMA

In the SoMa neighbourhood, visit the San Francisco Museum of Modern Art to take in the distinctive black-and-white central cylinder that divides its red-brick body. For now at least, Mario Botta's 1995 building stands alone, defiantly retro, but it will soon get a long-overdue expansion by Snøhetta, due for completion in 2016; call ahead as renovations will disrupt opening hours. The museum lies on an east-west axis and sunlight floods its circular skylight. Inside, as you would expect of such a structure, the galleries house a world-class collection of carefully curated contemporary art overviews and retrospectives. After a museum tour, recharge with a coffee at Caffè Museo (T 357 4500; closed Wednesdays).
151 3rd Street, T 357 4000,
www.sfmoma.org

19.00 Quince

The Bay Area is full of eateries run by excellent chefs who trained under slow-food queen Alice Waters at Chez Panisse (T 510 548 5525), but Michael Tusk is the current king of the pack and Quince is the jewel in his crown. In fact, many insiders consider it to be the best restaurant in San Francisco. In 2009, it moved from an intimate, 16-table spot in Pacific Heights to a large, historic building downtown. But although the vibe has changed (the old venue seemed a bit too exclusive; the new space is much busier), everything that made Quince great is present: unparalleled service and superb Italian- and French-influenced northern Californian fare made with local ingredients. Tusk's Italian restaurant, Cotogna (T 775 8508), sits adjacent to here and is a little more casual. *470 Pacific Avenue, T 775 8500, www.quincerestaurant.com*

URBAN LIFE

CAFÉS, RESTAURANTS, BARS AND NIGHTCLUBS

San Francisco's oceanside location and the verdant land outside the city mean that chefs here are blessed with some of the best raw ingredients in the US. The locals pride themselves on having an endless selection of exemplary eateries; from food trucks serving tacos to Michelin-starred restaurants turning out fine French fare with a Californian twist. Couple this with a reverence for good wine and experimental craft beers, and the result is that, whatever you crave, you'll be spoilt for choice. Excellent seafood, and Asian and Hispanic cuisine abound, but lately an Italian wave has swept the city, with cultish restaurants such as Una Pizza Napoletana (210 11th Street, T 861 3444) transforming simple ingredients and rustic fare into fetishised perfection. Reservations are de rigueur at most of the city's better venues but even so, be prepared to wait.

Great bars are as plentiful as the fog in this drinker's paradise. Some of them take a bit of seeking out, but idiosyncratic venues, such as Smuggler's Cove (650 Gough Street, T 869 1900) and Church Key (1402 Grant Avenue, T 986 3511), which has a stellar beer list, are worth the effort. The club scene is not immediately obvious either, or as open as in London or New York, but there are plenty of eclectic and interesting nights to be found. Follow our lead and, whether you're a dancing queen or a lounge lover, rest assured there's something in this city that will scratch your itch. *For full addresses, see Resources.*

Flour + Water

Featuring a handcrafted interior of reclaimed timber designed by Sean Quigley, owner of Paxton Gate (see p076), and walls hung with ethereal nature scenes and still lifes by local artists, this popular spot on the edge of The Mission has helmed the city's Italian renaissance ever since opening in 2009. As its name suggests, Flour + Water is devoted to the simple side of Italian cooking – no sodden ragus here. Instead, tuck into fresh, handmade pastas, thin-crust Neapolitan pizza and nose-to-tail meats cooked up by chef Thomas McNaughton, formerly of Quince (see p038). Look out for dishes containing honey from the restaurant's very own hive, such as the thyme *bonet* with strawberries and pistachio crumble. *2401 Harrison Street, T 826 7000, www.flourandwater.com*

Saison
Saison began serving its hyper-local
New American cuisine in 2009, earning
its first Michelin star two years later
and a second in 2012. The interior may
be average, but the food is a revelation.
Expect pure-and-simple meals with
ingredients like brassicas, wood pigeon
and Meyer lemons, crafted by Joshua
Skenes, who creates a new menu daily.
2124 Folsom Street, T 828 7990

Atelier Crenn

French chef Dominique Crenn named this restaurant after her father, whose artwork is displayed throughout, illuminated by striking wire chandeliers that resemble birds' nests. Crenn is renowned for her elegant plating, so try one of her tasting menus; either the five-course option or, to fully appreciate what she refers to as her 'poetic culinaria', the full 10-course, three-hour experience, paired with wine. The

Michelin-starred Atelier Crenn was the best place in San Francisco for foie gras before a city-wide ban came into effect in 2012, but its super-seasonal, vegetarian-friendly fare still draws large crowds.
3127 Fillmore Street, T 440 0460,
www.ateliercrenn.com

Nopa

A giant folk-art mural by locally based painter Brian Barnclo runs the length of Nopa's main wall, decorating two floors with scenes from San Francisco life. Matching the venue's boho vibe, the simple menu places an emphasis on wood-grilled and roasted meats and vegetables, handmade pasta and organic produce. This restaurant is a favourite with locals, who try to ensure it stays under the tourists' radar, so last-minute dinners here are a tall order. There is a big communal table where hopefuls who don't have a reservation wait it out; otherwise Nopa's sister eatery, the organic Mexican Nopalito (T 233 9966), is a block away. *560 Divisadero Street, T 864 8643, www.nopasf.com*

Outerlands

Within its weathered driftwood walls, this laidback restaurant near Ocean Beach serves up dishes such as cavatelli with wild mushrooms and kabocha squash. With its concise menu and fresh sourdough bread accompanying every meal, it's no wonder queues of hungry surfers stretch round the block.
4001 Judah Street, T 661 6140,
www.outerlandssf.com

Bourbon & Branch

This high-end whisky lounge manages to do the speakeasy thing without feeling gimmicky, mostly because the spot was actually an illegal den during Prohibition. Reserve a seat (and secret password) online for the main bar (opposite) or the detective-agency-themed adjoining room, Wilson & Wilson. Or just head to the Library (above); open from 6pm to 2am, Monday to Saturday, this hidden bar within a bar requires no reservation, and although Bourbon & Branch's full menu isn't available, its signature cocktails can be sampled. Plus, you still get the speakeasy thrill: ring the anonymous-looking buzzer and say the password 'books' for an escort. *501 Jones Street, www.bourbonandbranch.com*

Locanda Osteria

The latest Mission outpost of Craig and Annie Stoll's *nuovo-Italiano* empire, which includes the low-key but delicious Pizzeria Delfina (T 437 6800) a few blocks away, Locanda serves rustic, Roman fare. This includes guinea hen with pancetta and perfectly fried 'Jewish-style' exploded artichokes, alongside wood-fired dishes such as *pizza bianca* with bone marrow and radishes. Locanda opened in 2011 to a swirl of hype, and its opulently spare interior (gauzy drapery, modern geometric tiling) is often packed from wall to hearth with well-heeled San Franciscans 'slumming it' in The Mission. While you wait, hit the bar for the city's best negroni, made by Gabriel Lowe, formerly of Beretta (T 695 1199). Don't leave without a post-meal amaro from the venue's extensive liqueur list.
557 Valencia Street, T 863 6800, www.locandasf.com

Spruce

Opened in 2007, this New American restaurant in the elegant neighbourhood of Laurel Heights has an interior that is as inviting as its menu is appetising. Set in a restored former garage dating to the 1930s, the space is decked out with luxe interior touches, such as mohair sofas, a Carrara-marble bar, and limestone flooring salvaged from a French church. Chef/owner Mark Sullivan and his chef de cuisine John Madriaga, who cut his teeth at Manresa in Los Gatos and Noma in Copenhagen, serve expertly cooked ingredients from local farms, which earned Spruce a Michelin star in 2011. Try the Pacific sablefish with chorizo, black trumpet mushrooms and artichokes, or veal breast with English peas.
3640 Sacramento Street, T 931 5100, www.sprucesf.com

Sebo

Decorated with bamboo floors and moss green walls, this small but beautiful Hayes Valley venue is a bit slicker than your average sushi restaurant. The menu focuses on sushi and sashimi, made with extremely high-quality seafood. The only cooked ingredients here are in the six-course *omakase*, so if raw fish is not your thing you may want to reconsider. For sushi fans, however, it doesn't get much better. Star chef Anthony Bourdain even made a visit to Sebo on his TV programme *No Reservations*, adding to the popularity of the restaurant. Be warned, seats at the bar are walk-in only, so be sure to reserve one of the few tables in advance.
517 Hayes Street, T 864 2122,
www.sebosf.com

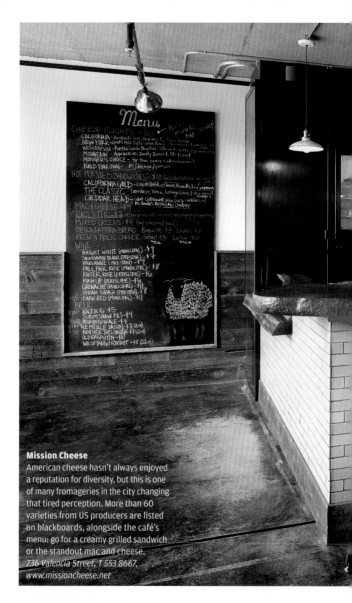

Mission Cheese
American cheese hasn't always enjoyed
a reputation for diversity, but this is one
of many fromageries in the city changing
that tired perception. More than 60
varieties from US producers are listed
on blackboards, alongside the café's
menu: go for a creamy grilled sandwich
or the standout mac and cheese.
*736 Valencia Street, T 553 8667,
www.missioncheese.net*

Press Club

There are plenty of wine bars in San Francisco, but only Press Club can offer a full wine-country experience in the city, which it delivers via a selection of more than 60 vintages from the best Napa Valley vineyards and beyond. In some respects, Press Club is a step up from the tasting rooms in Napa. Vintners from the area host weekly tastings, the food is delicious, its list of rare beers is, surprisingly, one of the best in town, and the decor – a Scandinavian-inspired wooden bar backed by a floor-to-ceiling display of bottles – is more diverting than that of the average Napa Valley winery. *20 Yerba Buena Lane, T 744 5000, www.pressclubsf.com*

The Brixton
The perfect balance between a swanky San Francisco bar and a traditional British pub, The Brixton serves classic cocktails and great food. One wall is covered in black-and-white wallpaper designed by street artist Shepard Fairey, while another is all windows looking on to bustling Union Street. *2140 Union Street, T 409 1114, www.brixtonsf.com*

Twenty Five Lusk
It can be hard to secure a table for dinner at this celebrity favourite, opened in late 2010, but the lounge (left) is where you'll want to be anyway. Designed by local studio CCS Architecture, the space retains a sense of the building's history – it was originally a 1917 meat-packing house – in a contemporary environment of steel beams and glass walls. In the lounge area, suspended fire pits and curved banquettes are dramatic and sexy, plus solidly poured drinks (including one of San Francisco's best Manhattans) get rave reviews; arrive at about 7pm to beat the crowd. If you happen to score one of the seats in the dining room, expect New American cuisine with a European slant, courtesy of Matthew Dolan, who trained with star US chef Emeril Lagasse.
25 Lusk Street, T 495 5875,
www.twentyfivelusk.com

INSIDER'S GUIDE

SARAH GREENBERG, JEWELLERY DESIGNER

Living and working across the Bay in Oakland, Sarah Greenberg regularly heads into San Francisco by ferry (T 510 522 3300, www.eastbayferry.com) to gather inspiration for her naturalistic, handcrafted jewellery line, Sarah Swell (www.sarahswell.com). Greenberg's perfect weekend-morning starts at Town Hall (342 Howard Street, T 908 3900), where she'll 'pig out' on Southern-style eggs Benedict. Sketchbook in hand, she often ventures to the Botanical Garden (1199 9th Avenue, T 661 1316) in Golden Gate Park, or to Russian Hill's lesser-known Ina Coolbrith Park (Taylor Street/Vallejo Street). 'I like working for my views,' she says, 'and here, you feel like you're at the top of the world.' A red potato, pesto and rosemary-topped slice of pizza from ZA (1919 Hyde Street, T 771 3100) fuels these urban hikes.

When Greenberg turns her attention to manmade treasures, she combs clothing and accessory boutique Candystore Collective (3153 16th Street, T 888 601 0117) or, on the first Sunday of the month, hunts for artefacts at the Alameda Point Antiques Faire (2900 Navy Way, T 510 522 7500). 'I'm there at 6.45am,' she says. 'I find props, pieces to cast and objects to inspire me.' When night falls, Greenberg attends concerts at The Fillmore (1805 Geary Boulevard, T 346 3000) or unwinds with a glass of mescal at the popular Mexican restaurant Nopalito (see p045).

For full addresses, see Resources.

ARCHITOUR

A GUIDE TO SAN FRANCISCO'S ICONIC BUILDINGS

San Francisco's first architectural golden age ended in rubble and smoke, when the 1906 earthquake and subsequent fire destroyed many of the city's Stick- and Queen Anne-style Victorian gems. Those that survived (see prime examples around Alamo Square and in The Mission's Liberty Hill) defined the city's past and its present – for years, new construction was stagnantly conservative.

Hope glimmered (despite the ridicule) with the Transamerica Pyramid (see p013) and Skidmore, Owings & Merrill's 1964 One Maritime Plaza (300 Clay Street). In 2005, Herzog & de Meuron's de Young Museum (see p070), finally changed the tide. Today, the Transamerica seems clunky compared with Morphosis' shiny Federal Building (see p014); the de Young has innovative company in the California Academy of Sciences (see p068); and Libeskind's diamond enlivens the Contemporary Jewish Museum (see p069).

Cultural venues represent the future. The rebirth of SFMOMA (see p037) began with Mark Jensen's Rooftop Garden, and its oft-mocked 1990s design will be transformed again when Snøhetta's expansion project begins in 2013. Meanwhile, Michael Maltzan is planning the sinuous Mashouf Performing Arts Center at SFSU's Lake Merced campus, and, nearby, Diller Scofidio + Renfro are at work on arts centres at Stanford and Berkeley – proof that the city is entering a new age of architectural exuberance.

For full addresses, see Resources.

St Mary's Cathedral

Architect Pietro Belluschi's cathedral is one of the Catholic Church's boldest 20th-century statements. Blessed in 1971, it has a travertine and concrete parabolic exterior, which rises from a square base to form a cross. The jaw-dropping interior emphasises this with stained-glass windows that ascend on four sides and converge at the apex. American sculptor Richard Lippold's 45m-high baldachin, made of more than 4,000 aluminium rods, is suspended above the altar. Soaring 57m from four concrete buttresses, the structure was realised by engineer Pier Luigi Nervi, and the overall impression is of both drama and serenity.
1111 Gough Street, T 567 2020 ext 207, www.stmarycathedralsf.org

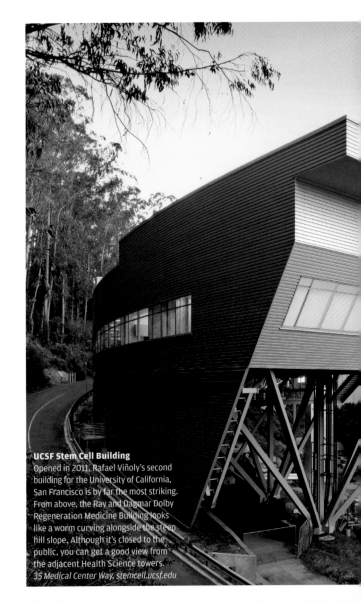

UCSF Stem Cell Building
Opened in 2011, Rafael Viñoly's second
building for the University of California,
San Francisco is by far the most striking.
From above, the Ray and Dagmar Dolby
Regeneration Medicine Building looks
like a worm curving alongside the steep
hill slope. Although it's closed to the
public, you can get a good view from
the adjacent Health Science towers.
35 Medical Center Way, stemcell.ucsf.edu

California Academy of Sciences

As if it wasn't enough to have the Herzog & de Meuron-designed de Young (see p070) in the middle of Golden Gate Park, Renzo Piano's California Academy of Sciences is just a few steps away, across the plaza. Best known for its undulating green roof and fantastic planetarium, the academy is one of the most environmentally friendly buildings in the United States. Not only is it energy- and water-efficient, it's also extremely functional. Which is just as well, considering the aquarium's fascinating collection of penguins, birds, butterflies, fish and alligators, which all need specific light and temperature conditions to survive and thrive.
55 Music Concourse Drive, T 379 8000, www.calacademy.org

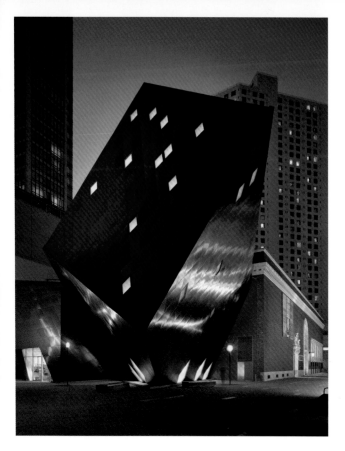

Contemporary Jewish Museum

Daniel Libeskind's Contemporary Jewish Museum, finished in 2008, incorporates an old power station that had to remain due to local planning laws. Libeskind's design was inspired by the Hebrew salutation *L'chaim*, which means 'To life', and the influence works on a number of levels: this was the city's main power plant (energy = life, geddit?); the new structure embodies the shape of the Hebrew letters that form the word *chai* (life); and the museum celebrates the art and history of the Jewish people. Rising up into two dark-blue steel triangles, one on either side of the building, it breathes life into the museum and the block it dominates. *736 Mission Street, T 655 7800, www.thecjm.org*

de Young Museum

The de Young is one of Herzog & de Meuron's most thoughtful projects. The building is covered in perforated and textured copper, which creates an impression of light filtering through trees. As the exterior ages and acquires its own patina, it will increasingly blend in with the park surroundings. Streams of windows and unexpected angles and apertures inside the building mean the inside and outside often feel blurred, but the galleries themselves are more conventional and let the art take centre stage. A 44m tower on the north-east side of the museum has a glass-walled observation deck, which affords great views over the park and the western side of the city. *50 Hagiwara Tea Garden Drive, T 750 3600, deyoung.famsf.org*

SHOPPING

THE BEST RETAIL THERAPY AND WHAT TO BUY

Union Square is the city's commercial centre and the location of department stores such as Macy's (170 O'Farrell Street, T 397 3333) and Neiman Marcus (150 Stockton Street, T 362 3900). In the surrounding streets, shopaholics can find pretty much all the name brands they want, from Marc Jacobs (125 Maiden Lane, T 362 6500) to Louis Vuitton (233 Geary Street, T 391 6200).

A foodie's paradise, San Francisco boasts a cornucopia of gourmet treats. Try Fog City News (455 Market Street, T 543 7400) for high-end chocolate, and Terroir (1116 Folsom Street, T 558 9946) for natural and biodynamic wines. The legendary Molinari Delicatessen (373 Columbus Avenue, T 421 2337), draws locals and visitors to its authentic Italian sandwiches. And the Rainbow Grocery Cooperative (1745 Folsom Street, T 863 0620) is possibly the most politically correct grocer you'll ever visit.

If it's obscure music you're after, Amoeba Music (1855 Haight Street, T 831 1200) is a must-visit. Located in a former bowling alley, the sprawling independent record store is a mecca for visiting musicians. For a more intimate feel, check out Aquarius Records in The Mission (1055 Valencia Street, T 647 2272). City Lights (261 Columbus Avenue, T 362 8193) bookstore is also a place of pilgrimage, as it was the epicentre of the beat movement on the West Coast. Poet Lawrence Ferlinghetti still holds court here. *For full addresses, see Resources.*

Lost Art Salon

This is one of those places that would have remained an insider secret before the advent of the internet. Despite the fact that many people have now discovered Lost Art, it retains an aura of mystery, partially due to its odd location on the third floor of the Sherman Williams Building. The gallery specialises in fine art and objects from 1900 to 1960, and is often tapped by prop stylists for film sets or by estate agents dressing midcentury-modern homes. Lost Art sells much of its inventory at very reasonable prices, and is also welcoming to those who just want to browse. Rugs are laid out on the floor and vintage couches are arranged amid a huge collection of modernist artwork, giving the place the feel of an intimate salon.
245 South Van Ness Avenue, Suite 303, T 861 1530, www.lostartca.com

General Store

Within earshot of the Pacific's crashing waves, this multifaceted boutique, located in the Outer Sunset neighbourhood, stocks everything a crystal-gazing, West Coast soul surfer could ever need, from vintage, Navajo-patterned Pendleton blankets and chunky, hand-knitted wool caps, to home accessories such as Luke Bartels' locally made rustic wooden chopping boards. Kathleen Whitaker jewellery, Postalco stationery and Morgan Parish leather goods line the store's walls and quirky wooden tunnel, built by architect Mason St Peter, who runs the place with his wife Serena Mitnik-Miller. If you want a piece of the beach habitat to take home, don't miss the local plants for sale in the desert-chic greenhouse, which was designed by artist Jesse Schlesinger and is tucked away in the backyard.
4035 Judah Street, T 682 0600, www.visitgeneralstore.com

Paxton Gate

Entering Paxton Gate is akin to discovering a Victorian cabinet of curiosities; this shop really is like no other in the city. From the museum-quality stuffed and mounted animal heads to the beautiful displays of butterflies, moths, spiders and beetles, through to the birds' nests, skeletons and who knows what else hidden in countless drawers, jars and cabinets, you'll be amazed and perhaps repulsed. Where else would you be able to pick up an owl-pellet analysis kit? If that's all a bit Darwinian for you, in the back is a greenhouse and nursery stocked with orchids and succulents.
824 Valencia Street, T 824 1872, www.paxtongate.com

Self Edge

Specialising in high-end raw Japanese selvedge denim (Iron Heart, The Flat Head, 3sixteen), Self Edge is worth a visit even if you're not in the market to drop a few hundred dollars on jeans. It stocks brands rarely found outside Tokyo (it also has a store in New York), and the variety is incredible, although there are definitely more options for men here than women. Free hemming, done with a vintage chain-stitching machine, is available on all jeans purchased in the store. The denim range is the focal point, but a good selection of men's shirts and accessories is also stocked.
714 Valencia Street, T 558 0658, www.selfedge.com

49 Geary Street

The five floors of 49 Geary Street are packed with some of the city's finest galleries. Each has its own feel and focus, although the majority are dominated by modern photography. The Bekris Gallery (above; T 513 5154), on the second floor, stands out for its emphasis on works from Africa, and for its range of disciplines; everything from sculpture to drawings to multimedia installations. Other favourites include: the Fraenkel Gallery (T 981 2661), which exhibits photography from the likes of Irving Penn; Stephen Wirtz Gallery (T 433 6879), which changes media with each exhibit; and Jack Fischer Gallery (T 956 1178), which focuses on self-taught artists. Many of the venues stay open late on the first Thursday of the month.

Park Life

Most major galleries have a decent gift shop, but it's unusual to find a good one attached to an independent art venue. Park Life, founded in 2006 by Derek Song and Jamie Alexander, puts equal emphasis on its two parts. In the rear is an exhibition space that has hosted shows such as 'Hyperspaces' (opposite), which included works from local artists James Sterling Pitt and Orion Shepherd, and in the front room (above), various art books as well as kitschy gift items, prints and DVDs are sold. Look out for Alexander Girard's wooden alphabet blocks, and the tomes published by Alexander and Song's imprint, Paper Museum Press. The shop opens at noon from Sunday to Thursday and at 11am on Fridays and Saturdays.
220 Clement Street, T 386 7275,
www.parklifestore.com

Monument

Hollywood Regency meets Eames-era modern at Monument, which carries a good selection of midcentury furniture, accessories and lighting. Here, Danish sofas, beautiful sideboards and original Hans Wegner pieces jostle for position with gilt-frame mirrors and Tommi Parzinger lamps. Owners Samuel Genthner and Michael de Angelis left their jobs at two well-respected San Francisco vintage furniture stores, X-21 and Bonhams respectively, to set up their own dream shop, so everything is sourced with passion. In 2009, Monument moved to its new 260 sq m venue, nearly twice the size of its original location next door, which has in turn been converted into an appointment-only space for collectors and designers, and showcases the store's best and most unique pieces.
573 Valencia Street, T 861 9800,
www.monument.1stdibs.com

William Stout Architectural Books
There's no telling how this bookshop, dedicated to architecture, art and design, stays open in this age of the superstore, but it doesn't seem to be going anywhere any time soon. Just a block away from the iconic Transamerica Pyramid (see p013), it was founded by architect William Stout. On returning from trips to Europe, and bringing back books unavailable in San Francisco, he found that friends would often ask him to acquire copies for them too. Today it is laden with piles of tomes that run the gamut of creative subjects, from typography and decorative arts to landscape and graphic design. The knowledgeable staff are always happy to answer your questions, help you find a text or leave you to browse.
804 Montgomery Street, T 391 6757,
www.stoutbooks.com

Carrots

Tucked away in a Gold Rush-era brick building near Jackson Square, Carrots is one of the best clothing boutiques in the city. Striking the perfect balance between high-end and accessible, it is constantly adding new lines from cutting-edge designers and international names, such as Rick Owens, Current/Elliott and Alexander Wang. The women's store stocks everything from T-shirts and cocktail dresses to shoes and jewellery. There's also a beautifully curated in-store apothecary packed with candles and fine fragrances, all sold with a smile by a team of staff on hand with advice, or, should you be in the mood, a carrot cupcake. *843 Montgomery Street, T 834 9040, www.sfcarrots.com*

Xanadu Gallery
Established in 1979, this eclectic
gallery, set just off Union Square in the
city's only Frank Lloyd Wright building,
stocks antiques and art sourced from
around the world. Specifically, Wright's
proto-Guggenheim houses artefacts,
artwork, textiles and jewellery from
Oceania, Asia and Latin America.
140 Maiden Lane, T 392 9999,
www.xanadugallery.us

SPORTS AND SPAS
WORK OUT, CHILL OUT OR JUST WATCH

The people of San Francisco are serious about sport and fitness, and with the topography of the city as it is, the daily walk to work can be akin to an intense StairMaster workout. It is obvious who the locals are, as they calmly stroll past the red-faced tourists huffing and puffing up the 1:3 inclines of the steeper streets. Cycle couriers here must surely give the Tour de France riders a run for their money, so, unless you're Lance Armstrong-fit, save the rental bike for crossing the Golden Gate Bridge (see p012).

There is an abundance of beaches in and around the city, and surfing is an all-consuming passion. The Pacific can be notoriously dangerous at San Francisco's Ocean Beach, which has frigid surf and powerful tides, but waves break softer a short drive away at Linda Mar Beach (see p090), and, a little further south, in laidback Santa Cruz. At Half Moon Bay, the legendary Mavericks wave break and its annual surf contest draws the world's biggest names.

Surprisingly for a US city this size, San Francisco doesn't have an NBA team – you have to go over the bridge to Oakland – so baseball and American football are the sports of choice. The concierge service at any of the better hotels should be able to procure tickets to a Giants (see p094) or 49ers (Candlestick Park, Jamestown Avenue/Harney Way, T 656 4900) game, which are always great spectacles, even for the uninitiated.

For full addresses, see Resources.

Mission Cliffs

If the near-vertical hills in some parts of the city aren't enough for you, this venue has it covered, whether you're a beginner or a regular rock jock. Mission Cliffs is operated by Touchstone Climbing, which now runs seven such indoor facilities in Northern California. This original and most impressive of its rock-climbing centres has a main wall that is more than 15m high, offering 140 roped routes – there are dozens more on the lower, boulder terrain. There's an upward path to suit everyone, but if you do lose your head for heights, the yoga studio and indoor cycling programme also guarantee a workout.
2295 Harrison Street, T 550 0515, www.touchstoneclimbing.com

Linda Mar Beach, Pacifica

Northern Californian surfing is different from Southern Californian surfing in many respects, but the major difference is the climate. Twenty minutes outside San Francisco, Linda Mar is a great surfing beach, both for beginners (typically in the morning; try Adventure Out, T 800 509 3954, which offers one-, two- and four-day beginner and improver surf clinics) and more experienced boarders.

Waves are mellow, but the weather isn't: fog and wind are as inescapable as the tide. A wetsuit is essential – Adventure Out will provide one if you book a lesson, or there are surf shops near the beach where you can rent one (and a board for that matter). Even if you don't surf, Linda Mar Beach is a great place to go, relax and watch everyone else hang ten.
Cabrillo Highway/Linda Mar Boulevard

Nob Hill Spa

Part of The Huntington Hotel (see p020), the Nob Hill Spa is one of the best that San Francisco has to offer. Its relaxation area, which surrounds an infinity pool, enjoys a panoramic view of the city. Treatment rooms may be feng-shui simple, but it's what happens inside them that's important: the spa is the only one in the city to offer Voya organic seaweed treatments. Its massage menu includes several hard-to-find therapies (Ashiatsu, dosha and Thai massage among them), and facials utilise effective brands such as Darphin and Baborganic, as well as LED light-therapy technology.
The Huntington Hotel, 1075 California Street, T 345 2888, www.nobhillspa.com

International Orange

In Pacific Heights, above the shopping bustle on Fillmore, International Orange provides a suitably Zen-like escape from the crowds. In addition to the spa's soothing crisp white walls, natural stones and wood floors, some of the city's best massage therapists and aestheticians are employed here. The spa stocks a first-rate selection of products, from the biodynamic Dr Hauschka line to the Hollywood favourite Arcona. Treatment rooms are small and the staff know their way around. To complete the relaxation package, yoga classes are offered daily in the spacious and airy studio (above). *2nd floor, 2044 Fillmore Street, T 563 5000, www.internationalorange.com*

AT&T Park

This is a city with a proud sporting history; those who have pulled on the jersey for the San Francisco Giants include baseball legend Willie Mays. If you can score tickets to a home game (slightly harder to come by since the team's 2010 World Series win), take a trip to AT&T Park in South Beach and revel in the atmosphere. Perched on the waterfront at the southern end of The Embarcadero, the views beyond the diamond and out to San Francisco Bay make this one of the most dramatic settings for Major League Baseball. If a slugger takes the plate and really connects, you might be lucky enough to see the ball go flying over the wall and into the McCovey Cove beyond, where enterprising kayakers gather with waterproof radios to listen to the game and paddle for 'splash hits'. *24 Willie Mays Plaza, T 972 2000, www.sfgiants.com*

ESCAPES

WHERE TO GO IF YOU WANT TO LEAVE TOWN

The countryside that surrounds San Francisco is some of the most beautiful America has to offer, the fault lines deep below causing a jagged, cinematic coastline and dramatic vistas. Leave the city in any direction and you will soon find yourself in epic surroundings.

A brief escape can be had by renting a bike and cycling north over the Golden Gate Bridge (see p012), either to the vista point on the far side, with its postcard views of the city (and consequent coachloads of tourists), or to the headlands beyond for more peace. If you're seeking a shady respite or a sublime connection with nature, make for Muir Woods (see p100), 19km north of Golden Gate Bridge. Although not a huge site, it's home to some coastal redwoods, which are among the tallest, most ancient trees on the planet, and can inspire Wordsworthian awe in the most confirmed of urbanites. One of the world's great drives is the journey south from San Francisco down the legendary Pacific Coast Highway to Carmel and Big Sur beyond, with the twisting, turning road taking you past the booming breakers of the ocean.

Heading in the other direction, north of the city, leads you to Sonoma and Napa Valley, and a dazzling array of vineyards (see p101). Thomas Keller's famous French Laundry restaurant (6640 Washington Street, T 707 944 2380; reservations essential) can be found in nearby Yountville, for those ready to splash some cash. *For full addresses, see Resources.*

Point Reyes National Seashore

There are myriad beaches and nature reserves outside San Francisco, but one of the most stunning is Point Reyes National Seashore. Only 50km north of the city, the landscape opens up into rolling vistas, which lead to huge beaches. Some, such as Stinson Beach, are family-oriented and suitable for swimming, whereas others, such as McClures Beach, are more dramatic, with treacherous pounding surf. The wildlife is abundant here, and includes pelicans, eagles and elk. Coastal walks, birding tours and sea kayaking trips can be arranged at Point Reyes Outdoors (T 663 8192). The grey whales' migratory path takes them up this coast, and at the right time of year, usually February, you can see them clearly from the historic Point Reyes Lighthouse (above) on the tip of the peninsula.

Hearst Castle, San Simeon
William Randolph Hearst's vast hilltop compound, which he named La Cuesta Encantada (The Enchanted Hill), may be a five-hour drive south, but it's a fascinating pilgrimage. One of the largest private houses ever built, it's unmissable if you swoon for displays of unbridled wealth. Book tours in advance. *750 Hearst Castle Road, T 800 444 4445, www.hearstcastle.com*

Muir Woods, Mill Valley

One of the enduring icons of California is the giant redwood, and some of the largest of these mighty trees are found in Muir Woods. Congressman William Kent and his wife, Elizabeth, bought the 247-hectare site north of the city in 1905, donating almost half to the government two years later to protect the trees from logging. In a further magnanimous gesture, Kent named the woods after conservationist John Muir, who described the honour as 'the best tree-lover's monument in all the forests of the world'. In an effort to protect the more venerable examples, there is now, alas, a manmade path, but the majesty of the trees when sunlight comes flooding through is impressive all the same. Arrive early to find yourself alone with some of the oldest living things on the planet. *T 388 2596, www.nps.gov/muwo*

Wine country

Despite the mockery of *Sideways*, don't be put off from taking a trip into California's wine region, where some of the most interesting varieties in the world are being produced. As a sample, we suggest driving north up Highway 121 to Markham Vineyards (T 707 963 5292), one of the oldest in the valley, to sample its justly famous merlot, then heading up to Rombauer Vineyards (T 707 963 5170),

to take in the amazing views from its glass-walled tasting room. Just down the road is Duckhorn (above; T 707 963 7108), one of the most forward-thinking vineyards in Napa, with its clubhouse-style tasting room. As you head back to the city, drop in on its sister winery, Paraduxx (T 707 945 0890), for a wine-tasting menu with hors d'oeuvre pairings, a fine way to round things off.

Monterey Bay Aquarium
Ninety minutes south of San Francisco
is arguably the country's best aquarium.
The considered, nostalgic architecture
of the building, on the site of an old
sardine cannery and featuring scores of
decks overlooking the ocean, is a winner,
and the diversity of aquatic species
will absorb keen Cousteaus of all ages.
886 Cannery Row, T 831 648 4800,
www.mbayaq.org

NOTES

SKETCHES AND MEMOS

RESOURCES

CITY GUIDE DIRECTORY

A

Adventure Out 090
T 800 509 3954
www.adventureout.com

Alameda Point Antiques Faire 062
2900 Navy Way
Alameda
T 510 522 7500
www.alamedapointantiquesfaire.com

Alcatraz Cruises 035
Pier 33
Hornblower Alcatraz Landing
T 981 7625
www.alcatrazcruises.com

Ame 025
St Regis hotel
125 3rd Street
T 284 4040
www.amerestaurant.com

Americano 027
Hotel Vitale
8 Mission Street
T 278 3777
www.hotelvitale.com

Amoeba Music 072
1855 Haight Street
T 831 1200
www.amoeba.com

Aquarius Records 072
1055 Valencia Street
T 647 2272
www.aquariusrecords.org

AT&T Park 094
4 Willie Mays Plaza
T 972 2000
www.sfgiants.com

Atelier Crenn 044
3127 Fillmore Street
T 440 0460
www.ateliercrenn.com

B

Bekris Gallery 078
49 Geary Street
T 513 5154
www.bekrisgallery.com

Beretta 050
1199 Valencia Street
T 695 1199
www.berettasf.com

Bliss Spa 018
W hotel
181 3rd Street
T 877 862 5477
www.blissworld.com

Botanical Garden 062
1199 9th Avenue
T 661 1316
www.sfbotanicalgarden.org

Bourbon & Branch 048
501 Jones Street
www.bourbonandbranch.com

The Brixton 058
2140 Union Street
T 409 1114
www.brixtonsf.com

C

Caffè Museo 037
SFMOMA
151 3rd Street
T 357 4500
www.sfmoma.org

California Academy of Sciences 068
55 Music Concourse Drive
T 379 8000
www.calacademy.org

HOTELS

ADDRESSES AND ROOM RATES

Clift 024
Room rates:
double, from $485;
Room 309, $475;
Studio Room, $505
495 Geary Street
T 775 4700
www.clifthotel.com

The Fairmont 016
Room rates:
double, from $250
950 Mason Street
T 772 5000
www.fairmont.com/sanfrancisco

Hotel Frank 022
Room rates:
double, from $150;
Deluxe Queen Room, from $150
386 Geary Street
T 986 2000
www.hotelfranksf.com

The Huntington Hotel 020
Room rates:
double, from $410;
Mulholland Suite, $1,300
1075 California Street
T 474 5400
www.huntingtonhotel.com

InterContinental 030
Room rates:
double, from $250;
One-Bedroom Corner
Suite 3006, from $750
888 Howard Street
T 616 6500
www.intercontinentalsanfrancisco.com

Mandarin Oriental 016
Room rates:
double, from $735
222 Sansome Street
T 276 9888
www.mandarinoriental.com

Mystic Hotel 017
Room rates:
double, from $160;
Mystic Junior Suite, $200
417 Stockton Street
T 400 0500
www.mystichotel.com

Orchard Garden Hotel 016
Room rates:
double, from $185
466 Bush Street
T 399 9807
www.theorchardgardenhotel.com

Palace Hotel 029
Room rates:
double, from $160;
Chancellor Suite, $1,000
2 New Montgomery Street
T 512 1111
www.sfpalace.com

Phoenix Hotel 016
Room rates:
double, from $130
601 Eddy Street
T 776 1380
www.jdvhospitality.com/hotels

WALLPAPER* CITY GUIDES

PHAIDON

Executive Editor
Rachael Moloney

Editor
Ella Marshall
Author
William Bostwick
Amy Westervelt

Art Director
Loran Stosskopf
Art Editor
Eriko Shimazaki
Designer
Mayumi Hashimoto
Map Illustrator
Russell Bell

Photography Editor
Sophie Corben
Acting Photography Editors
Anika Burgess
Elisa Merlo
Photography Assistant
Nabil Butt

Chief Sub-Editor
Nick Mee
Sub-Editor
Marie Cleland Knowles

Editorial Assistant
Emma Harrison

Wallpaper* Group
Editor-in-Chief
Tony Chambers
Publishing Director
Gord Ray
Managing Editor
Jessica Diamond
Acting Managing Editor
Oliver Adamson

Interns
Carmen de Baets
Lillian He
Despina Rangou

Wallpaper* ® is a
registered trademark
of IPC Media Limited

First published 2007
Second edition (revised
and updated) 2010
Third edition (revised
and updated) 2011
Fourth edition (revised
and updated) 2012

All prices are correct at
the time of going to press,
but are subject to change.

Printed in China

Phaidon Press Limited
Regent's Wharf
All Saints Street
London N1 9PA

Phaidon Press Inc
180 Varick Street
New York, NY 10014

Phaidon® is a registered
trademark of Phaidon
Press Limited

www.phaidon.com

A CIP Catalogue record for
this book is available from
the British Library.

ISBN 978 0 7148 6447 1

PHOTOGRAPHERS

SAN FRANCISCO
A COLOUR-CODED GUIDE TO THE HOT 'HOODS

NORTH BEACH
The north-east tip of the city boasts bars, restaurants, theatres and comedy clubs

NOB HILL
This affluent area is the place to come for some of the finest views of San Francisco

HAIGHT-ASHBURY
Follow the beatnik or hippie trail through this district and swing by the famous crossroads

SOMA
You'll find many of the city's best museums in this mind-broadening cultural hotspot

CHINATOWN
Fast-paced and fascinating, this is the largest and oldest Chinese enclave in America

THE CASTRO
On the West Coast's wildest gay scene, it's party central in the bars and restaurants

THE MISSION
Cutting-edge art, hip bars and designer stores have moved into the old Spanish quarter

HAYES VALLEY
Lined with quirky boutiques, this area's central street is a shopaholic's dream

For a full description of each neighbourhood, see the Introduction.
Featured venues are colour-coded, according to the district in which they are located.